INTRODUCTION

On August 9, 2018, at eleven years old, I was diagnosed with Type 1 Diabetes. Since then, every day I have become more inspired by how my body works. Nobody chooses to have Type 1 Diabetes, so everyone with this condition deserves to feel confident with themselves. That's why I decided to write this book. When I was first diagnosed with T1D I felt scared and overwhelmed. But after a few days, I became more empowered and secure. So, I wrote "From My Eyes" with the hope to help kids, like me, understand how to manage diabetes easily and feel comfortable with themselves.

1. CHECKING YOUR BLOOD SUGAR

You are going to have to check your blood sugar 4-6 times per day. I am going to teach you all you need to know! When you are recently diagnosed with diabetes your blood sugar will be going up and down, up and down, and again. Don't worry that is normal! You want to always have candy that is at least fifteen carbs, or glucose tablets, with you in case your sugar drops. Your blood sugar is low when you are at 70 or below. Your blood sugar might be high because you ate more than what you bolused for, or because your insulin dose may have to be recalculated by your doctor.

> I usually carry 3 Starbursts with me just in case my sugar drops.

SURVEY #1

1. What goal numbers did the doctors give you?
Day:
Night:

2. How do you feel about measuring your blood everyday?
a. It's fine
b. I'm scared
c. I'm mad
d. I feel...

3. From 1 to 10 how much did it hurt the first time?

4. What finger are you most comfortable using?

2. INJECTING INSULIN

I remember thinking this was going to be the hardest part. Partly because I was terrified of needles, and also because the thought of having to do this every time before I ate was very annoying. Now, for me, this is the easiest part. I have an app on my phone that does all the calculations for me (it is called "BolusCalc"). These injections don't hurt at all! They become part of your day. The doctor gives you two different insulin pens. One is for the night and the other one is to bolus for a meal.

> Injecting faster is the best way!

SURVEY # 2

1. What are the names of your two pens?

2. How many units of long acting insulin do you inject at night?

3. Do you do it by yourself?

4. Where are you most comfortable injecting?

5. On a scale of 1 to 10 how much does it hurt?

3. GOING BACK TO SCHOOL

Telling your friends is hard, but I recommend telling them before going back to school. Your friends will support you all the way, which is why it is important for them to know. It is completely normal to be nervous. A good tip to do this is having one of your best friends, if you choose to tell them first, help you (it helped me). You can do it through a text, a call, in person, one by one, or however you feel most comfortable. Remember to be confident! When you go back to school you might feel like there are eyes on you, but remember that you are the same person you were before. You do not look any different. It is all in your head. People will not stare, and if they do remember you are rock star! You are brave, and that is what people think when they see you.

I texted my friends to let them know.

SURVEY # 3

1. How did you tell your friends?

2. How did your friends react?

3. Are you confortable with them knowing?

4. How was going back to school?
a. It was Ok
b. Great!
c. Could have been better, because...

5. Was it easy to go back to school?

4. THE HONEYMOON PHASE

The honeymoon phase is just what it sounds like! It is a period in which your body is using the bits of insulin it can still find. Usually, during this phase your blood sugar remains pretty stable. This phase sometimes lasts six months, one week, two months, or maybe even much longer. No one knows exactly how long it lasts. However, staying active and eating healthy is a good way to help it last. Some days during your honeymoon phase you might not have to inject insulin at all!

5. THE SENSOR (DEXCOM)

The Dexcom is your friend. You don't have to have it, but it makes your life easier. The Dexcom is a tiny sensor that you stick on to your body with a small pinch, it does not hurt at all. The Dexcom automatically measures your blood sugar every five minutes, and sends a loud notification when your blood sugar drops or when it rockets up. The Dexcom comes with instructions on how to put it on and use it.

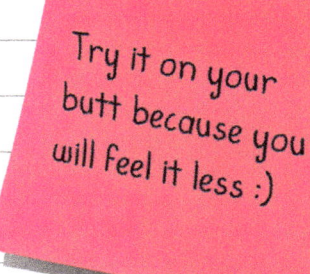
Try it on your butt because you will feel it less :)

6. EMOTIONS

    Yes, it will be stressful., and yes, it will be hard. But do not hold back. Cry if you need to cry, and be angry if you need to be angry. All of your emotions fall into one place, if you do not let your sad and angry emotions out, your happy and excited emotions will not come out either. You are not "strong" if you do not cry... Everyone cries, so does that mean no one is strong? No, strong people cry when they need to cry, and when a moment comes to be happy they are the happiest.
    Sometimes it feels better to let your emotions out with someone you care about. It can be a friend, a sibling, a parent, a cousin, or anyone!

> I usually speak with my parents

SURVEY # 4

1. Is it easy for you to let your emotions out?

2. What do you do when you feel angry?

3. Who do you like to speak to about how you feel?

4. Use this space to write how you feel about having Type I Diabetes.

7. ABOUT FOOD

Even though you can eat whatever you want, it is always best not to eat too many carbs. Even though you inject yourself the insulin for what you are eating, it is never 100% exactly what you need. So, if you eat a large amount of carbs it is likely that your blood sugar will go high and then really low. This is why it is always better to stay carb smart! When you are about to eat analyze your plate and ask yourself, "Is this carb smart?" or "Is this meal good for me?" Be kind to your body, make smart choices, and stay healthy!

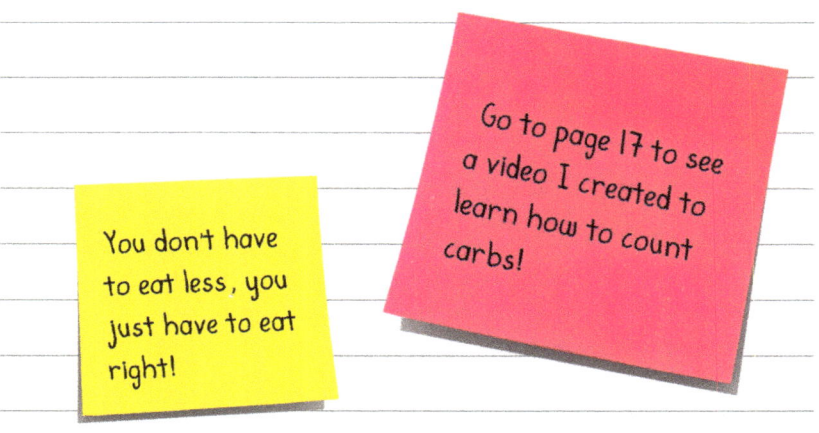

You don't have to eat less, you just have to eat right!

Go to page 17 to see a video I created to learn how to count carbs!

8. THE SKY IS THE LIMIT

Diabetes will not stop you from doing ANYTHING! The sky is the limit! If you like sports and you want to be an athlete, Diabetes will not stop you. In the beginning, you might begin to think that diabetes is going to prevent you from doing many things, but this is not true. Diabetes only makes you stronger, because now you are more conscious of your body and what you are eating. No matter what anybody says, you just remember... The sky is the limit!

ACKNOWLEDGEMENTS

There are so many people that I would like to thank, I don't know where I would be without them. Let's start with my Mom, not only did she help me download everything I wrote and drew about this book to the computer, but she gives me her unconditional love and support everyday, and everyday she does more Diabetes research to help me. My dad, he also gives me his unlimited love and support everyday, when my blood sugar is low he's the first one to call me no matter where I am. My amazing doctors, Lizette and Dr. Nemery. They are without a doubt the best doctors I can ask for. Lastly my friend Nikki who is also a Type 1. The day after I left the hospital she came to my house to help me and give me a kid's perspective on Diabetes.

ABOUT THE AUTHOR

Veronica Halfen was born November 9, 2006 in Caracas, Venezuela. Two years later she moved to Miami, Florida with her family. She has two siblings, an older brother (Eduardo) and a younger brother (Alexander), and her parents Stephanie and Ricardo.

She has always loved to write and draw, so making this book has been a great adventure! She loves having fun with her friends, playing many sports, and doing all kinds of outdoor activities. She also loves cooking, photography, and making videos.

BACK COVER ANSWERS!

- What did I do to get Type One Diabetes?

    Absolutely nothing! Unfortunately doctors still don't know why someone might get T1D, but what they know for sure is that nothing you did caused it.

- Did I get it because I ate too much sugar?

    No, you don't get T1D because you ate too much sugar.

- If I have T1D can I eat sugar?

    Yes, but try to have your limits.

- Is T1D contagious?

    No, it is not.

If you have more questions you can write me at:
vero.frommyeyes@gmail.com

INTERACTIVE VIDEO

Learn to count carbs with me!
Scan this QR code :)

NOTES...